As if I Couldn't!

Collection of poems
for small and grown-up children

by

Bohumila Ottová

Illustrated by Katarina Bikard

AS IF I COULDN'T!

Welcome, welcome, don't be shy!
Flick a page or two,
Read,
Give it a try…

Copyright © 2024 Bohumila Ottová
Illustrations copyright © 2024 Katarina Bikard
All rights reserved.

ISBN: 9798300290580

WORKS BY BOHUMILA OTTOVÁ

STORIES AND POEMS IN ANTHOLOGIES

Ayrshire Stories: Tales from the West Coast, 2024
The Paul Cave Prize for Children's Literature 2024
Jigsaw Pieces, The Greats in Flash Fiction,
An Oxford Flash Fiction Prize Anthology, 2024
A Collection of Verse, Volume II, TS Publications, 2024
Ageing, an Anthology of Poetry and Short Stories, 2024
But Words Can Never Hurt Me, The Greats in Flash Fiction,
An Oxford Flash Fiction Prize Anthology, 2023
The Paul cave Prize for Literature, Short Stories,
Flash Fiction and Poetry, 2023
Brouhaha, the Winning Short Stories, Writefluence, 2023
Of Heartbreaks and Subdued Yearning and Other Winning
Stories, FemmeFluenza, Writefluence, 2023
In Times of Sorrow,
an Anthology of Poetry and Short Stories, 2023
It Was a Queer, Sultry Summer, Writefluence, 2023
Death and Grief, Anthology of Poetry and Short Stories, 2023
Crimson and Other Winning Stories, Writefluence, 2022
Short Stories from Strasbourg, Top 20 Stories, 2020
Short Stories from Strasbourg, Top 20 Stories, 2019
More Short Stories from Strasbourg, Top 20 Stories, 2015

POEMS, STORIES, ARTICLES IN MAGAZINES

All Your Stories, August 2024
All Your Poems, August 2024
All Your Stories, June 2024
All Your Stories, Editor's Choice, April 2024
All Your Poems, February 2024
All Your Poems, December 2023

POEM COLLECTION IN CZECH

As if Nothing, Just So by Bohumila Ottová and Libuše Matýzková

AS IF I COULDN'T!

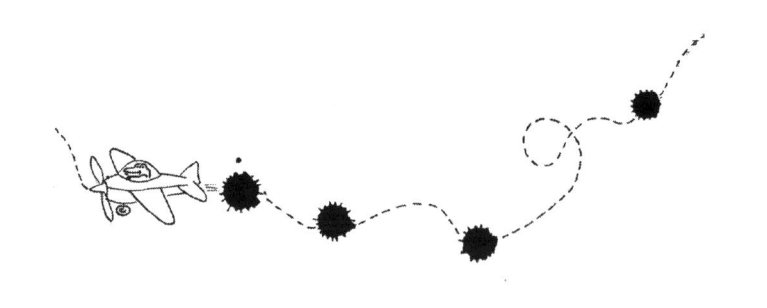

AS IF I COULDN'T!

DEDICATION

To my beloved children Matia and Nathanaël.
To my nieces, nephews, children of my friends and all those that brightened and brighten my life.

To Claudia, Paul and Saul Bragman.
To Eleanor, Alice and Charlotte Garside.

My biggest thank you goes to my mum, who taught me the beauty of poems.

To Aaron Mullins, guiding me on every step of the way.
I wouldn't make it without your unwavering support.

To Alexandra Ross, my dear friend and first reader.
To Julia Weston, to whom I am grateful
on so many levels!

To my inspiring dear friend Katarina Bikard.

To Sorcha O'Connour, Louise Barton, Denise Donio, Alicia O'Callaghan and all those whom God has placed upon my path and without whose encouragement this book wouldn't exist.

To my teachers Mr Trojan, Ms Bartoňová, prof. Kaněra and prof. Šuchová, who believed in me.

To our poetry club and its intrepid leader
Valentyna Kryvenkova.

Special thanks go to Vedran and Louise.

… AS IF I COULDN'T!

AS IF I COULDN'T!

CONTENTS

Ink Blot 5

Music Box Ballerina 6

A Hungry Mountain 7

French Beans 8

Yum, Yummyyyy 9

Jimmy the Kangaroo 10

Spinach for Supper? 12

As You Do 13

A Racing Snail-drive to School 14

Stephen 15

My Baby Brother's Very Big 16

Toby the Pirate 17

Good I Don't Fish 18

Getting Dressed 20

When You Smile 21

I'm Being Followed! 22

A disaster in a Tin Castle 23

Amy the Ladybug 25

George the Monkey 26

Swimming Like a Dolphin 28

The White Rabbit 29

AS IF I COULDN'T!

Clumsy Anda Panda 30
Calypso the Naughty Cat 31
Theo the Porcupine 32
Snail Pet at the School 33
I Am Not Always Right, Though Often I Might 34
The Little Monster's Scared of Me 35
Your Brown Eyes 36
I Just Can't Go to Sleep 37
My Super Duper Dad 38
Dizzy from the See-Saw 39
Creepy Crawly friends 40
A Happy Loser 42
A Dare Disclaimer 43
Tongue-Twist with Me 44
Whichever Whoever? Whatever. Whenever & Wherever.
.... 45
Whatisitthatyouare? 46
Cooking with Magic 47
Shenanigans 48
Stories That Are Yet To Be Written 49
Cat on My Lap 50
I Wish I Could Sleep in 51
I Am Sick 52

AS IF I COULDN'T!

Back to School 53

Little Jane* 54

A Shopping Expedition 55

The Train's Song 56

Petey Went to the End of the World.................................57

What Would You Do?..58

Sister and Brothers from Other Fathers............................60

Fluffy Bear 61

A Dream House 62

A "Black Paws" Mystery 63

Don't Say "I Can't!" 65

To Ace the Basket Case 66

Blocked. *Knock!* 67

I Want to Be a Knight 68

A haircut...69

Cherries after the Storm 70

To Act or Not to Act Like a Girl...72

As if I Couldn't!...73

About the Illustrator 75

About the Author 76

Thank You...77

Follow Me 78

Support Me 78

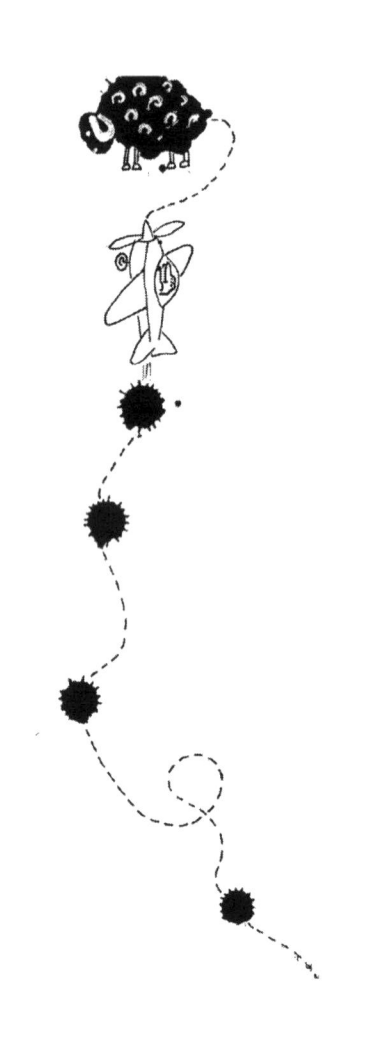

AS IF I COULDN'T!

INK BLOT

Whether you believe me or not,
I saw this magic ink blot.
It jumped off my fountain pen
across the page, away it ran.

It was changing all the time
Into a frog, a crocodile
Into a cowboy or a plane
Into a sturdy puffing train.

It grew the wings and soared up high
making splashes in the sky.
The clouds turned into running sheep,
that you count to fall asleep.

The magic ink blot worked so hard
that the whole sky grew stark dark.
The moon then lit up every star
so you can see near or far.

For you to find your little bed
the star garland above it spread.
The ink blot's settled in his nest.
Sleep, my love. Now get some rest.

MUSIC BOX BALLERINA

The Ballerina from the music box
tore up her dress, lost her socks.
The music played.
She was dancing still,
exposed to the winter chill.

Now she's got a runny nose,
which alters her gracious pose.
I gave her a dressing gown,
and so she rests, the lid pulled down.

A HUNGRY MOUNTAIN

Hoppity, rockity
Hoppity, rock
A mountain ate clouds
and spat out some rocks.

Hoppity, rockity
Hoppity, whea
The mountain drank rain
and spat out blue sea.

Hoppity, rockity
Hoppity, whish
The mountain ate pebbles
and spat out fish.

Hoppity, rockity
Hoppity, wrum
"For all that work done,
Here's a hug,"
Said the Sun.

FRENCH BEANS

I don't like French beans.
Mum doesn't understand
when I blanch.

But I just can't eat greens
that only speak French.

YUM, YUMMYYYY

One, two, three
A marshmallow tree.

Four, five, six
Liquorice sticks.

Seven, eight, nine
Lollipops to dine.

Ten, eleven, twelve
If I could reach the shelf!

JIMMY THE KANGAROO

Jimmy the Kangaroo
Skipped out of the ZOO.
He hopped onto the road
and met Charles the Toad.

They hopped across a bridge,
Stopped at the 7-Eleven fridge.
Peter Pan who works there
employs Barry the Polar Bear.

He makes the ice cream they crave for.
They bought all he had in store.
Tomorrow they'll come back for more.

AS IF I COULDN'T!

SPINACH FOR SUPPER?

I don't like spinach,
It's mucky and yucky.
I hope the fish tank
will hide it well.
I hope I'll get that lucky.

AS YOU DO

Some days I am feeling sad.
On such days, I can tell you that
I jump, I smile and look for sun.
Striving to be happy,
that's easier said than done.

I enjoy each sip of tea.
I stroke a bark of a tree.
I hug my friends and family.
I smile more and happily.

I jump and dance a little bit.
People say: "Wow, today you're fit!"
And at the end it is true.
I turned it 'round; as you do.

A RACING SNAIL-DRIVE TO SCHOOL

We're in the starting blocks.
My racing snail put on his racing socks.
I sat atop, in front of his house,
waiting for a signal from Sam the Mouse

My school bag and a lunchbox are ready.
I clutch on to his eyes to keep steady.
One, two, three: salute!
We're off, we're on the route.

STEPHEN

Stephen, Stephen
To get even
As you ate
My grandma's cake
I think I'll try
your mummy's pie.

MY BABY BROTHER'S VERY BIG

My baby brother is very big,
his legs through our main door stick.
His hands through windows, reach to town.
He wears the house roof like a crown.

The chimney looks
like a feather on a hat.
And don't get me started on
when he needs to be fed.

TOBY THE PIRATE

Toby the Pirate
Jumped onto the plank.
Made a somersault.
Into the sea sank.

Or so he thought.
He bounced on a whale,
'n got sent back on the boat
with a swoosh of
the whale's tail.

GOOD I DON'T FISH

Good I'm no fisherman
and I don't fish.
Had I caught a golden fish,
no clue what I'd wish.

AS IF I COULDN'T!

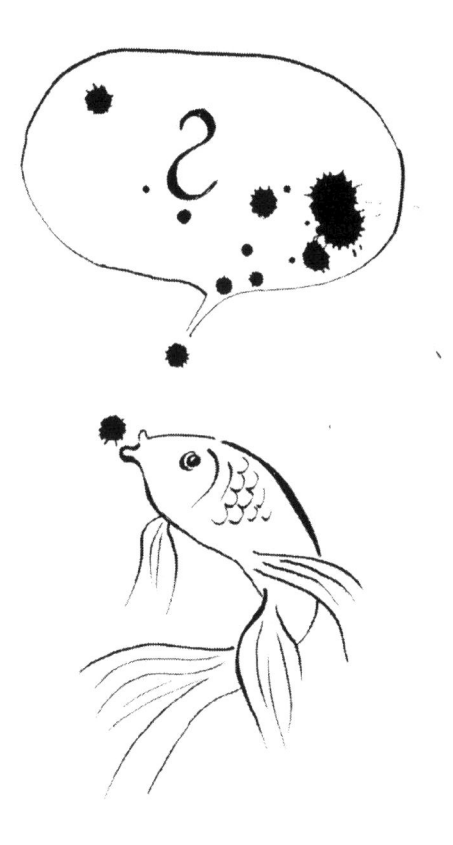

GETTING DRESSED

I donned a brand-new shirt.
I put on a new red tie.
I donned a new straw hat.
So elegant am I!
I put on new leather shoes.
New orange socks and I
cannot really get it why
everyone laughs so wild.
Even my good friends:
Oh, I'm not wearing any pants!

WHEN YOU SMILE

When you smile
The sky is blue.
When you sing
I feel it too.

The grass gets green
with kangaroos.
Lions turn red
in the zoos.

When you laugh
an angel sings.
When you dance
sun golden-beams.

When you kiss me
I'm in smithereens.
You're my rainbow.
You're all my dreams.

I'M BEING FOLLOWED!

Be it in glee
or in sorrow,
Where I shall go
he will follow.

Stuck to my side
as if with glue,
Where I shall go
He will go too.

In the sunshine
Under a gas lamp
Whether it's warm
or cold and damp.

Stuck to me fast.
I swear it's true.
Whatever I do
My shadow'll do too.

A DISASTER IN A TIN CASTLE

Lily, Charlie and George
Isla, Theo and Tim
They worked.
and worked,
and worked.
Built a castle made of tin.

There were no windows.
There was no door.
There was no furniture.
They sat on the floor.

There was no roof.
But that's alright.
For it is summer,
sun's shining bright.

But then Alfie, Theo's dog
rushed after a little frog.
He raced through the castle hall,
through the chambers.
That's not all!

He ran, he sprang, he fooled around
and brought the castle to the ground.
What a racket from falling cans.
So many tears from destroyed plans.

AS IF I COULDN'T!

Lily, Charlie and George
Isla, Theo and Tim
Cried a lake, full to the brim.
Then jumped in for a wee swim.

AMY THE LADYBUG

Poor Amy, the Ladybug
got sick with a nasty bug.
When in fever, getting hot
she lost one cherished dot.

As she was getting hotter
mummy called for their doctor.
"Switch on a ventilator
I am sending you a painter."

Doctor arrived on the spot,
greeted t' painter, Mr. Scott.
Paint has dried on Amy's back.
All relieved, they took a snack.

GEORGE THE MONKEY

George the Monkey
went to town.
He found a crown
laying on the ground.

He put it on his head
and one man said:
"It must be a king,
since he has a crown!"
So, all around
just knelt down.

AS IF I COULDN'T!

SWIMMING LIKE A DOLPHIN

I like swimming like a dolphin
or jumping like a frog,
stalk-walk like a stork.
But what really bums me out?
Is having to just walk.

THE WHITE RABBIT

The white rabbit's running late
He's got so much on his plate!
Besides meeting Cheshire cat,
he has to clean his tall hat.

Do make sure you hurry too.
Drink up, eat up, as you do.
Forget all you thought you knew.
Today's magic's coming through.

CLUMSY ANDA PANDA

Anda Panda clumsy klutz
Broke all plates and all the cups.
She tried to juggle on a ball
but fell down and broke it all.

CALYPSO THE NAUGHTY CAT

Claudia, Paul and Saul
Play with a kitty cat down the hall.
That naughty kitten munched Claudia's mitten.
That naughty cat chewed on Paul's hat.
And chose Saul's slipper for a bed.

The little kitty cat seems a little mad
for she wakes up when they go to bed.
She bounces, jumps and hunts
on shadows, fridge, or grunts.

She gets mad and she gets moody.
Even with their Auntie Judy.
Why are they all lying in bed?
Are they sick? Or are they sad?

Kitty cat has to find that out
by biting their toes,
planting its claws
in their chests, thighs, or hands.
She must have the evidence that stands.

Claudia, Paul and Saul
Will not sleep well at all.
And in the morning, when it's time to play?
Kitty cat's tired. Will sleep the whole day.

THEO THE PORCUPINE

Theo the sweet porcupine
has been invited to dine.
He brought with him on his back
fruits for everyone to snack.

SNAIL PET AT THE SCHOOL

Don't bring your snail pet to the school!
He'll slow you down and he'll drool.
And his homework -unlike mine-
is like goo; covered in slime.

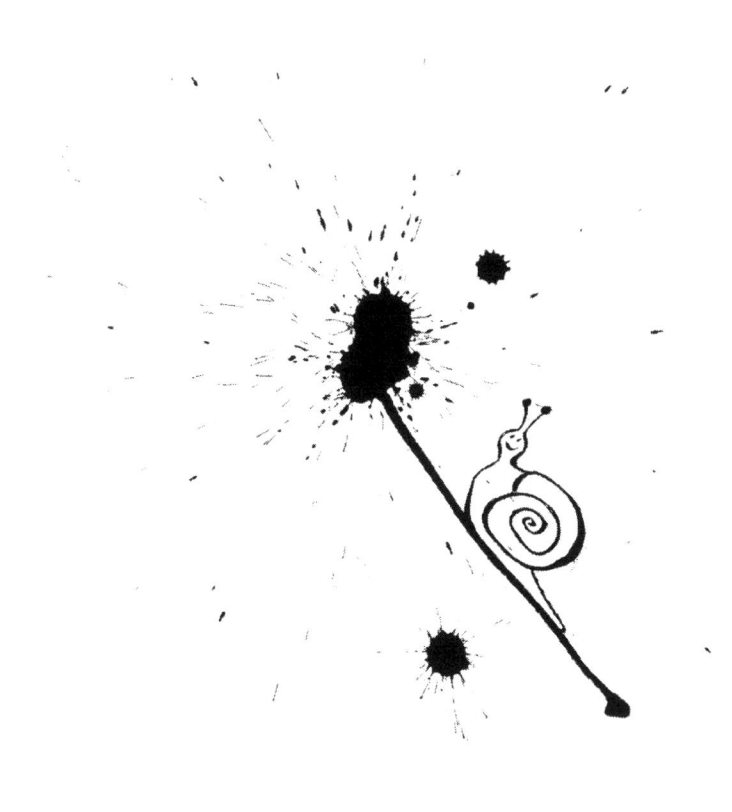

I AM NOT ALWAYS RIGHT, THOUGH OFTEN I MIGHT

I'm not always right.
I might even be wrong.
But the chance I'm right
is very very strong.

THE LITTLE MONSTER'S SCARED OF ME

The little monster is scared of me
when I sleep or drink my tea.

He is scared of my brown eyes,
of my plaids, and of my size.

When he sees me, he just cries
and repeats the "oh-why-oh-whys."

Mama monster pats his head.
Even when he wets his bed.

She goes: "Shh, shhh, little lamb,
shall we build you a wee tent?"

"Daddy monster'll watch the gate
Now go to sleep. It's pretty late."

YOUR BROWN EYES

Your brown eyes are shining bright,
Bringing laughter into the night.
Bringing warmth and cuddles too.
It's all as true as I love you.

I JUST CAN'T GO TO SLEEP

Mum wants me to go to sleep,
but my ship would sink too deep.

Mum says I should go to bed,
but my dragon has to be fed.

I should have a wee lie down,
but what if the sky broke down?

What if the giants fell to the ground
and in the sky-blue grass got drowned?

The cloud sheep can't swim.
I can't leave it to mum's whim.

You see why I can't go for a nap.
'Cause all'd turn out pretty bad.

MY SUPER DUPER DAD

My dad is stronger than five men,
wrestles a lion in his den.

He juggles rhinos on his nose,
and lifts up two bears on his toes.

If robbers see him, they will frown,
apologise and leave the town.

The monsters tiptoe out of sight,
go cry to mama: "What a plight!"

Dad kills a dragon every noon
just with the back of his little spoon.

But when mum calls out: "Lunch!"
My dad might almost swoon.

He hurries and calls back:
"My love I'll be right there.
Quicker than soon!"

DIZZY FROM THE SEE-SAW

I love the see-saw.
It's like a dance
of the air, the wind, the *whoosh*.

I love the see-saw
when dad's pushing me.
It's like on an air cruise.

I like also when I get off
and my legs are shaky.
As if I'd got off a boat,
I'm feeling a wee bit flaky.

Daddy will give me piggyback,
and I will feel so tall.
We'll eat pancakes for a snack.
That's the best of all.

CREEPY CRAWLY FRIENDS

Can you see Mummy
the bright star on the right?
The one that shines really bright.

That's Jody the Spider
and her best friends.
They're together,
holding hands.

She weaved a fine rope
of her cobweb string,
and they dance together
in a ring and sing.

There's Jody the Spider,
Pete the Centipede,
Amy the Ladybird,
and her cousin Bert.

There's Ian the Cricket.
There's the Grasshopper James.
There's the Dragonfly Rufus
and the Cockroach Pams.

I'm sure the astronomer
looking at them now
can't tell it's just friends
having fun.

AS IF I COULDN'T!

He'll call it Ursa Major, Orion or something else.
It's our secret they are *really*
creepy crawly friends.

A HAPPY LOSER

I am a sore loser,
say Ma and Dad.
But I'd like to see anyone,
whom losing doesn't make sad.

I throw the board game in the air.
The pieces fly up high.
It's a new game
I've just made up.
And this one
makes me smile.

A DARE DISCLAIMER

To read these poems out loud
might be quite a feat.
For some of them are
pretty hard to read.

TONGUE-TWIST WITH ME

A big black bear sat on a big black rug.
He didn't really care; seemed quite smug.

"Thin sticks, thick bricks"
The three little pigs learnt some new tricks.

Ed took notes and had edited it, for he knows
the hunter threw three (not four) free throws.

We surely shall see the sun shine soon,
said the cow, who jumped over the moon.

She said she met a ponytailed Rory,
Who kept saying: "Red lorry, yellow lorry."

But now she doesn't say it anymore,
as she sells seashells by the seashore.

WHICHEVER WHOEVER? WHATEVER. WHENEVER & WHEREVER.

Whoever wrote to Whichever a letter.
Whenever asked, "Whoever'll know better?"
Whoever answered on this serious matter:
"Whatever you do, don't take off your sweater.
Wherever it rains, you'll just get wetter."

WHATISITTHATYOUARE?

Where do you live?
In a fountain pen's nib.

Where are you from?
Where the stories are born.

What do you eat?
Lovely words, that's a treat.

What do you drink?
Dark blue pen ink.

Who are you then?
A poem from the pen.

COOKING WITH MAGIC

If you dipped
your pen nib
into dip, gravy, or sauce,
wrote a recipe,
and sim sala bim!

Would it turn
into a main course?

Well yes.
Of course!

SHENANIGANS

I like the word "shenanigans."
It makes my mouth and mind dance.
I don't know though what it means.
Maybe a bag of spilled beans.

STORIES THAT ARE YET TO BE WRITTEN

How many stories are hidden in an ink well?
I don't know yet. But it's time to tell
the beginning, the middle and the end.
Will you help me by listening, my dear friend?

CAT ON MY LAP

I went to bed.
Onto me my cat leapt.
Settled on my lap
and purred.

I wanted to nap,
but with the cat on my lap
I haven't dared.

I WISH I COULD SLEEP IN

I wish I could sleep in,
and play all the games I didn't play till end.
I wish I could sleep in
and learn how to see behind a bend.

But I've to go to school.
Get up, get dressed. Oh dear!
I wish mum was so cool
to say: "School?
No way, keep clear!"

I AM SICK

My head hurts,
I cough and spit.
My stomach burns
because I'm sick.

Mum tucks me in bed,
strokes my hair.
Kisses my forehead.
She'll always be there.

I sometimes fake
being sicker than I am.
Then when asleep or awake
I can have kisses, hugs,
and toast with strawberry jam.

BACK TO SCHOOL

I can't wait to go back to school
and see again my friends.
I do like the holidays
but also when they end.

LITTLE JANE*

Little Jane
from down the lane
bought a magic hat.

When it was sunny,
it grew a bunny,
thought it'd stay at that.

When it was foggy,
it grew a froggy.

When it was chilly
she acted silly.

When it was cold
it made her look old.

But one day
a gust of wind and rain
blew it off
and it sailed down the drain.

We've never seen it again,
Nor the little Jane.

---

* First published in the *Paul Cave Prize for Children's Literature 2024, Flash Fiction, Poetry and Short Stories,* Tim Saunders Publications.

A SHOPPING EXPEDITION

Rickety rockety golbilly whop
I pull my cart to the Main Street shop.
Instead of a bag, I took a big bowl,
put in it the flour, milk, eggs, and all.

Rickety rockety golbilly whop
I'm on my way from the Main Street shop.
The road is rickety rockity stone
up the hill, down the hill, all the way home.

I run and run at a break-neck speed
to bring to my mum all she might need.
But I spilled the milk, I broke the eggs
on the rickety rockety golbilly tracks.

To make sure mummy doesn't get cross,
I pull out the bottle, the paper bag tossed.
Hugging my mum, smiling like a sun,
I say: "Tada! The batter is done."

THE TRAIN'S SONG

I like the song of the train.
Tudum tudum bdam
I could take it every day.
Tudum tudum bdam

I like how it gently sways,
Tudum tudum bdam
like a film the nature plays.
Tudum tudum bdam

You can read or play a game.
Tudum tudum bdam
It will never feel the same.
Tudum tudum bdam

Will you one day join me too?
Tudum tudum bdam
Pretend we're the railway crew?
Tudum tudum bdam
Tudum tudum bdam.

PETEY WENT TO THE END OF THE WORLD

Off Petey Pete set
For the end of the world.
It's been quite a while...

But the world is round
like a nice ball of yarn.
The end's hard to come by.

Unless the world is
a huge ball of wool
of a giant knitting granny.

And she knits it off
into a pair of socks
and there won't be left any.
Not even the size of a penny.

WHAT WOULD YOU DO?

What would you do if you had a hole in a shoe?
I'd patch it with a handful of the sky-blue.

What would you do if you bumped your head?
I'd plaster to it a slice of bread.

What would you do if the house was on fire?
I'd climb on a cloud and sail much higher.

What would you do if waters washed you away?
Then I'd find an island where I'd like to stay.

What if you were there all alone?
Then I'd find a magic stone.

And I'd wish everyone and everything as before
With or without shoes, a bumped head and all.

I'd just like you to tuck me in my bed.
Even if we lived in a garden shed.

As long as we're all there.
About the rest, I don't care.

AS IF I COULDN'T!

SISTER AND BROTHERS FROM OTHER FATHERS

You're my sister from another mister.
You're my brothers from another father.
Whether we say it out loud or in a whisper,
You're my brothers, you're my sister.
There's nothing else to add further.

FLUFFY BEAR

Where do you sleep fluffy bear?
What is that you call a home?

In a den, right over there,
just at a throw of a stone.

What do you play fluffy bear?
Who are those bears all around?

I juggle the apples and a pear
with the best friends that I found.

What do you eat fluffy bear?
Why did you switch off the light?

Whatever there is to share.
Then I bid all a good night.

A DREAM HOUSE

One little
Two little
Three little mice
Ran up the clock,
down the clock
in a rickety croockety
small mushroom house.

The windows of pepper
The salami door
The roof of tomatoes
rolled over the floor.

The chimney of parsley
The walls made of cheese.

One little
Two little
Three little mice
Have always dreamt of these.

AS IF I COULDN'T!

A "BLACK PAWS" MYSTERY

I spotted black stains
on the kitchen floor.
One, two, three, four
and many more.

They were dark.
They were wet.
I braced myself,
on a mission I set.

I follow the trail
my heart beating fast.
I admit I am scared,
now that you ask...

I walk slowly
so as not to scare
the thief, the pirate, the witch
that might be there.

Through the hall to the bathroom
I tiptoe, holding my breath.
If this is where it ends,
I need all my strength!

AS IF I COULDN'T!

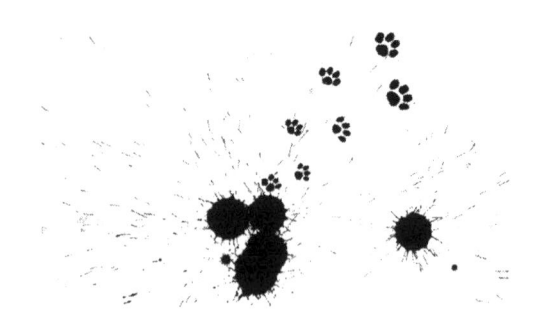

The door is ajar
I poke in my head
It's not a witch, a monster.
It's something else instead.

On the tiles sits
with colour-stained paws
a little black kitty cat
with a lovely pink nose.

DON'T SAY "I CAN'T!"

You know what I don't like?
When you say to me: "I can't."
There are forbidden things.
That is true.

But when you are good,
when you are kind to everyone,
There is nothing you might not do.

TO ACE THE BASKET CASE

I went to a market,
bought myself a basket.

Poured in it some water.
Brought it to my doctor.

It is because I care
I brought you some fresh air.

I brought you a new shirt.
Cleaned it well in the dirt.

I brought you also some burr
to mess up your fair hair.

I brought you muddy mud
so you can wash your butt.

And I'll give you a pence
to find in it a sense.

BLOCKED. *KNOCK!*

Knock, knock!
"The shop is closed!"
Knock, knock!
"The door is locked."

Knock, knock!
"The blinds are down."
Knock, knock!
"We're out of town."

Knock, knock!
"Now will you stop?"
Knock, knock!
"But I am blocked.
You closed the door on my frock!

And I haven't got all day
to stay here, knock and pray.
Open please and let me pee.
Then I swear, I'll let you be."

I WANT TO BE A KNIGHT

All I want is to be a knight;
Fight the evil, set things right.

Save the prince from the dragon's keep,
Kiss him if he's fast asleep.

Sail for cure to a distant land.
With the kingdoms, friendships mend.

I'm as smart as any other,
Beat at chess my older brother.

I can fight and I can rest
if you'll have me as a guest.

There's nothing really, I can't do.
Save to sit still. That is true.

A HAIRCUT

Mum says I need a haircut.
And that she won't hear a "but".

But have you ever seen
A pirate with hair clean?
With my hair nicely trimmed
Pirates wouldn't be thrilled.

They'd be laughing.
They would scream.
They'd make me rub
the deck clean.

They'd pour the dirty water
over my head.
Mummy, how would you like that?
I'm sure you wouldn't be glad.

I'll comb my hair without protest.
Can we forget about the rest?

CHERRIES AFTER THE STORM

I like the cherries. But what bad luck
When the thunder our tree struck
To run away from the storm
In each cherry hid a worm.

AS IF I COULDN'T!

TO ACT OR NOT TO ACT LIKE A GIRL

Lou, cover that scratched knee.
You're not acting like a girl!
Ladies don't climb in a tree,
They smile, in a dance they twirl.

I don't want to be a girl,
And even less a lady.
I don't want to wear the pearls.
A slingshot would be handier.

I would like to be just me.
Let people call it what they like.
Why not just have some fun
Can we ride a motorbike?

You see, the point is *that*
I'd like to be me. Not just act.

AS IF I COULDN'T!

As if I couldn't jump into puddles.
As if I couldn't play for long hours.
As if I couldn't climb a tall tree.
As if I couldn't brave any sea.

As if I couldn't sling a good shot.
As if I couldn't flee, not get caught.
As if I couldn't play the same games.
As if I couldn't break off the chains.

As if I couldn't run in the rain.
As if I couldn't jump off a train.
As if I couldn't play with flames.
As if you couldn't grasp it, James.

Me too, I can climb over the garden door,
Be a pirate or like a lion roar.
I love adventure, have courage for four.
I'm not *just a girl*. I'm so much more!

AS IF I COULDN'T!

ABOUT THE ILLUSTRATOR

Katarina Bikard

Meet Katarina: an artist with an eye for finding beauty in the grey of everyday life. With a paintbrush in hand, she usually depicts pigmented worlds of colourful flowers: from their emerging buds to their decaying blooms.

Her art is synonymous with life and colour - hence why this collection of black and white drawings was therefore somewhat of a challenge. Albeit one she welcomed with open arms.

The playful illustrations accompanying Bohumila's poems all used random ink blots, scattered across the paper, as a starting point.

They represent both the mistakes and frustration a child might feel as they learn how to write, as well as the messiness of a happy childhood spent jumping into puddles or splashing paint all over the walls.

She hopes the unpredictable drawings remind us to appreciate the simple beauty and humour of life's fleeting moments.

ABOUT THE AUTHOR

Bohumila Ottová

I am a false grown-up. I look like one, but my head and heart are filled with stories and adventures, and I still like stepping into puddles or splashing around.

I wanted to grow-up, so that I wouldn't have to have a nap.

I wanted to grow-up, so that I wouldn't have to do homework.

I wanted to grow-up when a friend was mean.

I wanted to grow up, so that I could do what I want.

I did grow up. And I would like to be small again, to do all those things I didn't like then. But if you grow in your body and keep on dreaming, I suppose that's still fine.

THANK YOU

Thank you, thank you,
for reading till the end.

Come again, alone,
or bring with you a friend.

Bohumila Ottová

FOLLOW ME

Instagram: bohumila_ottova_author

Amazon:
https://www.amazon.com/stores/Bohumila-Ottova/author/

SUPPORT ME

Did you like this book? Then don't hesitate to recommend it to your friends and/or to follow me, so that you are the first one to learn when there's a new book coming out.

https://bohumilaottova.wordpress.com/

Printed in Great Britain
by Amazon